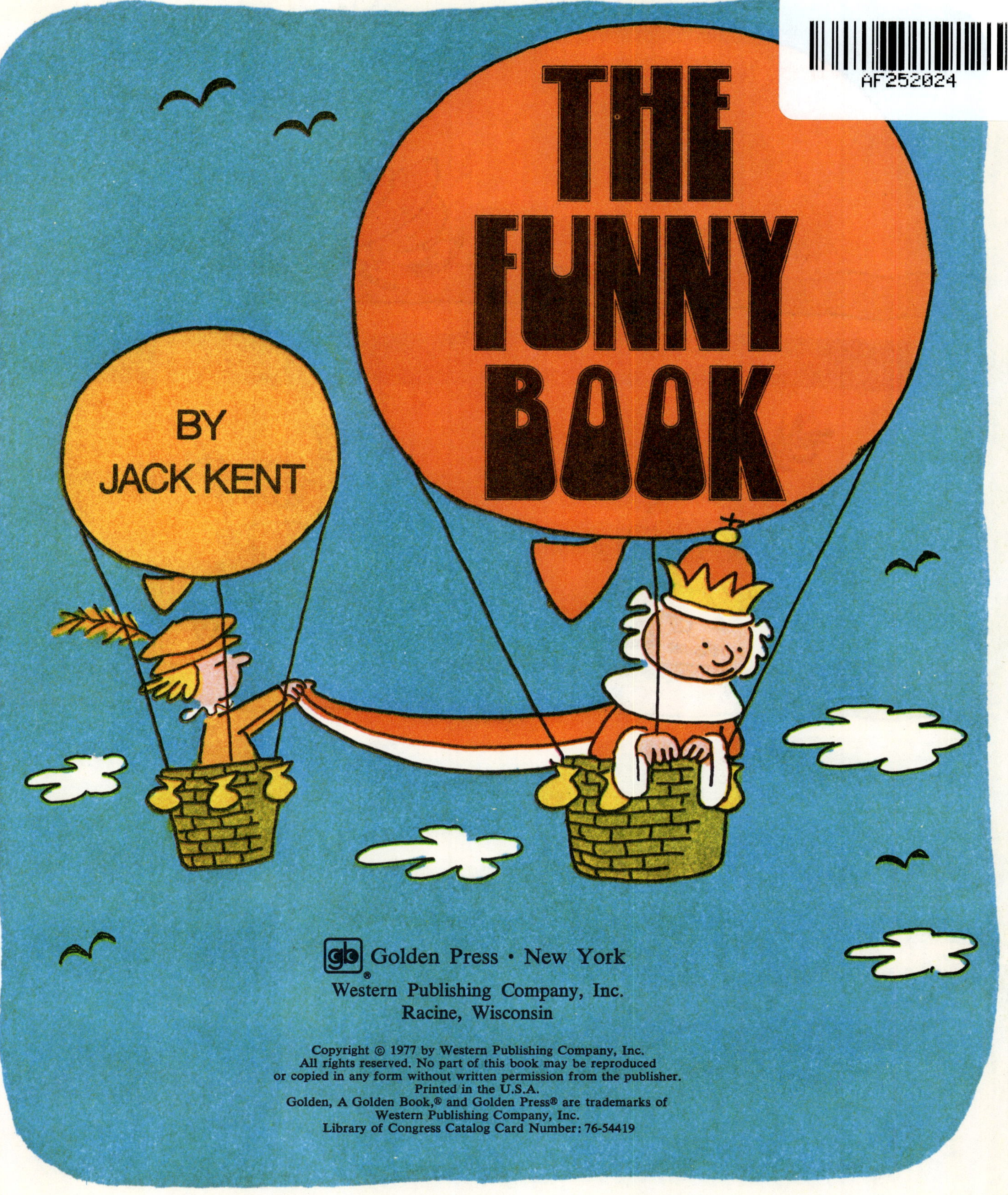
THE
FUNNY
BOOK
BY
JACK KENT
Golden Press • New York
Western Publishing Company, Inc.
Racine, Wisconsin
Copyright © 1977 by Western Publishing Company, Inc.
All rights reserved. No part of this book may be reproduced
or copied in any form without written permission from the publisher.
Printed in the U.S.A.
Golden, A Golden Book,® and Golden Press® are trademarks of
Western Publishing Company, Inc.
Library of Congress Catalog Card Number: 76-54419

Where do cows like to go on a Saturday night?

To the moo-vies.

When are cows apt to be especially restless?

On moo-ving day.

Where do cows stay overnight?

At a moo-tel.

What do you call Alaskan cows?

Eskimoos.

Looner Doctor: Ask the accident victim his name so we can notify his family.
Looner Nurse: He says his family already knows his name.

Mrs. Looner: I don't want the same kind of flour you sold me last week.
Looner Grocer: What was the matter with it?
Mrs. Looner: It was so tough we couldn't eat the biscuits I made with it.

One day, Tracy Looner went to see a fortune-teller.

"Welcome to my tent," said the fortune-teller. "I will answer any two questions for ten dollars."

Tracy thought for a minute and then took out a ten dollar bill.

"Isn't ten dollars a lot of money for just two questions?" she asked as she handed the bill to the fortune-teller.

"Yes, it is," answered the fortune-teller. "And now, what is your second question?"

Why did it take three Looners to help the old lady across the street?

She didn't want to go.

Farmer Looner: What are you doing up in my chestnut tree?
Little Looner: Nuttin'.

What's big, gray, and has horns?

The Elephants' Marching Band.

How can you tell when there is an elephant hiding under your bed?

When you are nearly touching the ceiling.

How do you keep an elephant from going through the eye of a needle?

Tie a knot in his tail.

Why aren't elephants allowed on the beach?

They can't keep their trunks up.

What's the similarity between an elephant and an aardvark?

Neither one can water-ski.

Who is beautiful, gray, and wears glass slippers?

Cinderelephant.

What's gray, weighs two tons, and has wings?

Cinderelephant's fairy godmother.

Who started the elephant jokes?

That's what the elephants want to know.

What animal can jump higher than a house?

Any animal. A house can't jump.

Mabel Looner: I never go to the store without forgetting something.
Mary Looner: What did you forget this time?
Mabel Looner: I forgot to go.

Why did the ghost go to the doctor?

He needed a boo-ster shot.

Roger: My dog took first prize at the cat show.
Steve: How was that?
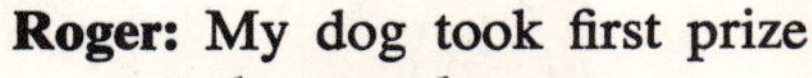
Roger: He took the cat.

DENTIST
BUILDING
COMING
DOWN

DENTIST
BUILDING
COMING
DOWN

W
S
N
E
BUILDING
COMING
DOWN

N
E
BUILDING
COMING
DOWN

DOWN
UP
LOW
CLEARANCE

TAXI
57¢ FIRST MILE

MARSH-
MALLOWS

Where do sheep get their hair cut?

At the baa-baa shop.

How do sheep like to drink their soda pop?

From the baa-tle.

Why don't they use glasses?

Because they think washing up is too much baa-ther.

Carol: Did you know that it takes three sheep to make a sweater?
Edith: I didn't even know sheep could knit.

What did the picture say to the wall?

First they frame me, then they hang me.

Hostess: Why do you set your tea on a chair, Mr. Jones?
Guest: It was so very weak, ma'am, I thought I would rest it.

A man ran into a hardware store. "One mousetrap, please, and hurry," he said to the clerk. "I have to catch a train."

"I'm sorry, sir," said the clerk. "We don't have any traps that big."

Why did the Looner parents keep their baby on the record player?

Because it had an automatic changer.

Motorist: I'm terribly sorry. I've run over your cat, but I've come to replace him.
Owner: Well, that's very thoughtful of you, but can you catch mice?

City Looner: How much milk does that cow give?
Farmer Looner: She don't give none. What you get, you have to work hard for.

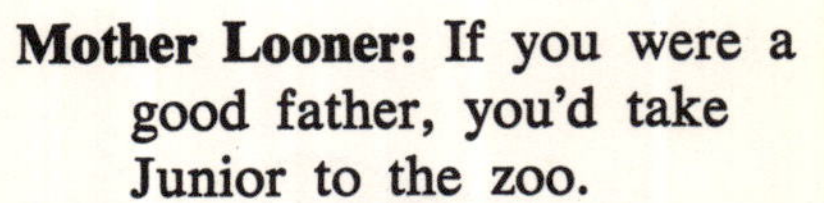

Mother Looner: If you were a good father, you'd take Junior to the zoo.
Father Looner: Nothing doing! If the zoo wants Junior, let them come and get him.

Where do ghosts get their hair done?

At the boo-ty parlor.

Roger: Did you hear the one about the three eggs?
Pat: No.
Roger: Two bad.

Jack: My family thinks there's something wrong with me because I like waffles.

June: There's nothing wrong with that. I like waffles myself.

Jack: Oh, do you? You must come over to my place sometime. I have seven trunks full of them.

Two doctors met at a convention.

"Max!" cried one. "I haven't seen you in years. You sure have changed. You used to have thick hair, now you're bald. You used to be fat, now you're skinny. You used to be short, now you're tall. You never had a mustache before, now you've got a real bushy one."

The other doctor answered, "But my name isn't Max."

"So!" cried the first doctor. "You've changed your name, too!"

What is the disease most feared by ghosts?

Boo-bonic plague.

Anne: What's the difference between an elephant's trunk and a mailbox?
Carrie: I don't know, you tell me.
Anne: I'm not going to tell you, but I'm not going to send you out to mail a letter either.

DID YOU HEAR
THE ONE ABOUT
THE THREE WELLS?
NO.
WELL,
WELL,
WELL!
!

BANG
BANG

BANG

How do you keep a dog out of the road?

Put him in a barking lot.

Why did the cow wear sneakers?

Because her platform shoes were in the repair shop.

Mother Looner: Lucy, have you finished filling the salt shakers?

Lucy Looner: Not yet, Mother. It's hard pushing the salt through these little holes.

Ben: It's unpossible!

Kathy: You mean impossible, don't you?

Ben: I mean it can't be did!

What's a nice present for a baby ghost?

A pair of boo-tees.

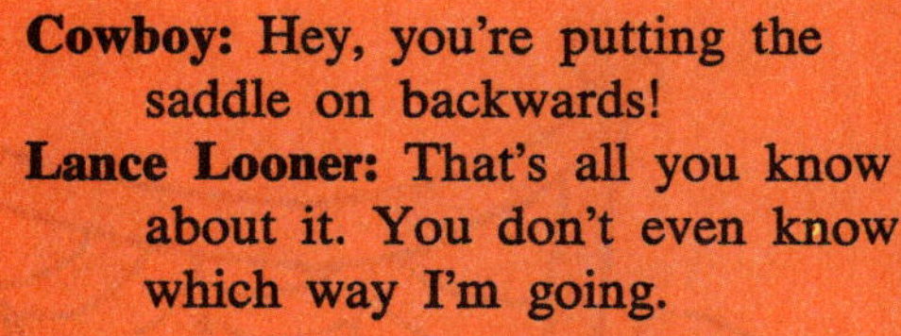

Cowboy: Hey, you're putting the saddle on backwards!
Lance Looner: That's all you know about it. You don't even know which way I'm going.

What do you call a rabbit with a lot of fleas?

Bugs Bunny.

Which president wore the largest shoes?

The one with the largest feet.

Customer: This diner must have a very clean kitchen.
Manager: Thank you, ma'am, but how did you know?
Customer: Everything tastes of soap.

WHO DREW THAT?
teechuR

What do aardvarks have that no other animal has?

Baby aardvarks.

Doctor: Has that insomnia medicine I prescribed had any effect yet?
Patient: Well, my foot was asleep this morning.

THE END
OF THE WORLD
IS NEAR

"My apartment is just too crowded," complained Art. "I wouldn't mind the whole family living with me if it weren't for their pets. My brother John has five dogs and my sister Kathy has nine cats. When they start chasing each other, it frightens my sister Janet's four monkeys. They get to screeching and wake up my nephew Jamie's ten geese. What a racket, especially with all the windows closed."

"Why don't you open the windows, then?" asked his friend.

"What?" cried Art. "And let my thirteen buzzards escape?"

When shouldn't you try to land on the moon?

When it's already full.

What's the difference between a full moon and a half moon?

30,000 tons of green cheese.

Why are there no monkeys on the moon?

Because there are no bananas.

George: Well, Peggy and I have managed to furnish three of the six rooms in our house by getting furniture with the soap coupons we collect.

Derrick: You've furnished three whole rooms by collecting soap coupons? That's great! Will you be trying to furnish the other three?

George: Oh, no. They're full of soap.

What scuffles around all day and sits under the bed at night with its tongue hanging out?

A shoe.

Je ne comprends pas.

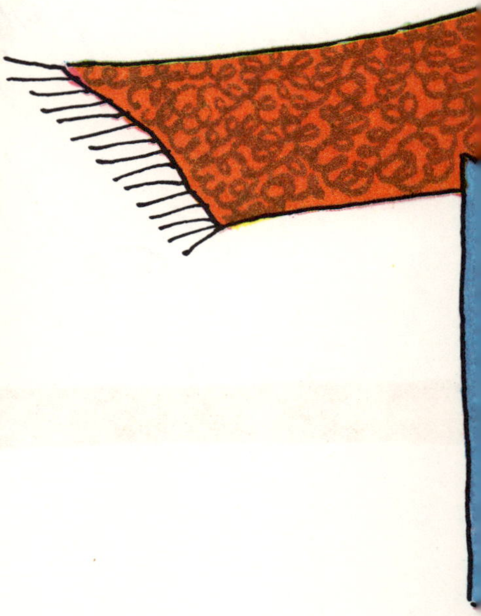

Mr. Looner: Gee, I'm glad I wasn't born in France.
Mrs. Looner: Why?
Mr. Looner: I can't speak a word of French.

Looner: I'm glad they named me Larry.
Friend: Why?
Looner: Because that's what everyone calls me.

NO SMOKING
DURING TAKE-OFF,
SIR.
REX

ECHO POINT
ECHO POINT
ECHO POINT
ECHO POINT
SNOW WHITE IS THE FAIREST IN

THE END